I0407622

Blame it on Obama

THE MISTAKES AND SUCCESSES OF THE OBAMA PRESIDENCY

Dr Markeith Porter with Irma Porter

ISBN: 1545278180

ISBN 13: 9781545278185

Library of Congress Control Number: 2017905653

CreateSpace Independent Publishing Platform

North Charleston, South Carolina

Introduction

Blame it on Obama—everything, nothing, or something? Trump's victory? Hillary's defeat? Immigration? The economy, the national debt, Iran's and North Korea's nuclear programs? You'll have to read this book and make your own decisions. That is what this book is about: inviting—and allowing—you to make your own decisions.

The eight years of Barack Obama's administration ended with the inauguration of Donald Trump as the forty-fifth president of the United States, which was followed by intense national turmoil, debate, and angst—significant in our lifetime but not unprecedented in American history. Who's to blame?

In authoring this book, I jumped at the chance not to sway others to my opinion but to demonstrate respect and cooperation with a person who has opinions and views different (some diametrically) from my own.

I agreed to author this book to demonstrate that it is possible to separate another's opinion from the content of his or her character. I consider myself humble, intelligent, and compassionate—all traits to admire. The acceptance of another's opinion without denigration is the attitude I pray that our country will take away from witnessing these issues without losing the respect and admiration we have for one another. The capability to listen without hatred is critical for the citizens of this great nation to make the best possible decisions to move our country forward as it has moved through countless periods of uncertainty. Join us as we debate the question: Should we blame it on Obama?

Chapter One

Trump Is the Legitimate President of the United States

Some may say that nothing could be further from the truth than that Donald Trump is the legitimate president of the United States. I don't agree.

Republicans would have you believe that Donald Trump should be accepted as legitimate simply because he won the electoral vote. This is the same man who conjured up false stories about President Barack Obama's birthplace. Consider this for a moment.

Donald Trump is a lot of things, and he is legitimate as president, but let me tell you what Donald Trump is not legitimate as. He is not legitimate to the Muslim community because he attacked Islam based on a few radicals. You may ask when he did such a thing. For starters, he selected members to serve in his cabinet who have reputations such as Flynn and Bannon; there are others, but this book is not dropping names.

The first person to hire me was a Muslim American at Taco Bell. She told me I did not have many skills for the job, but her dad told her to help military members any chance she could. She hired me, and I excelled at the position because I was thankful to her, and I appreciated her confidence in me. I was a dishwasher, and I approached dishwashing with the same vigor I approach most tasks with.

Donald Trump is not legitimate to the LGBT community because of his wishes to roll back all the gains during the Obama administration. You may say, "When did he say such a thing?" He positioned men in his cabinet who promulgate his agenda on what can only be called a radical website, Breitbart.

I remember serving with a chief who served with distinction in the field of intelligence communication. He made chief in eight and a half years and master chief in thirteen years. I do not think his sexual orientation had any bearing on his talents to do his job and serve his country.

Donald Trump is not legitimate to those who are most vulnerable in that he mocked the disabled. All my life, I was taught to fight for those most vulnerable, the disabled, and yes, blacks. I was taught to never make fun of the disabled because you never know when you might be in the same situation. The commonness of a stroke could render you disabled in seconds. I was horrified by the bully absolutely making fun of a disabled person. This alone should make Donald Trump illegitimate.

Donald Trump is not legitimate to the black community for falsely conjuring up and ridiculing John Lewis, an American hero of the civil rights movement. Also, he did not have to agree with John Lewis, but no one can doubt his contribution to every American's civil rights. He called the man all talk and no action, knowing the man was beaten at Selma, Alabama. To call the man such vulgar things is shameless. In addition, I think he did irreparable harm to some black youths in New York by saying that they raped a white woman. Even after the courts exonerated the youths, he still promulgated their guilt. This was yet another shameful act by a man so desperate to be better than Obama.

You see, Obama broke many of the norms that white men such as Donald Trump held. These stereotypes that many whites have of blacks in America are not reality for many black Americans. It is a television version of black Americans being criminals and always up to mischief.

Donald Trump is not legitimate to Mexican Americans for his stance on documented immigrant children. To state that you will send these young, talented children back to a country that they are not familiar with is immoral.

I guess what I am trying to say is that Donald Trump is the legitimate president of the United States, but is he the legitimate president of the people? This will only be answered in time. When I mention the people, I mean those referred to in the Constitution: "We the people...in order to form a more perfect union. We are endowed by our creator with certain inalienable rights." As a former member of the military, I hold firm that I will protect and defend the Constitution against all enemies, foreign and domestic.

Chapter Two

Willie Horton

When the Republicans ran the Willie Horton ad, they knew exactly which audience they wanted to connect with to extract the exact reaction they wanted. White males were horrified by the image of this black man who went to prison for rape and was let out only to kill and rape another person. He killed a white woman. The call for stiffer penalties was on from that point onward.

Under Obama, mandated sentences were no longer the mantra for justice. He reduced the "three strikes and you are out" law for drug-related crimes. The significance of the Willie Horton commercial had much to do with law and order. Contrary to popular belief, Democrats support the concepts of law and order. However, we also see certain crimes as compassionate issues too. Ferguson and Trayvon Martin were our modern-day Willie Hortons, conjuring up the idea of the raging black monster looming in the neighborhood from whom we must protect our white women.

No matter the issue, law and order should prevail—not just for black men but for all men and women. I think back to my mother's style of discipline; it was riddled with the concepts of law and order. The first time I stole a dollar out of my mother's purse, she whipped my bottom something fierce. She had one of those double-braided switches used in the South so that when you bruised, it would appear smaller. This was very effective. I can remember jumping around, trying to get away from the beating. I learned much about law and order in those beatings. There was no "three strikes and you're out" rule. One could only imagine if my mother had given me punishment such as standing in the corner until she was ready for me to move. I think it would have been easier to absorb. I think I would have stolen again, hoping for the same punishment. I think I would have had a sense that I was invincible, and I would have stolen a third time. The first time my mother had severely beaten my bottom, I would have thought she was crazy. She did not seem to care much about the situation that occurred two times before. I hope you follow the logic.

Her compassion to me is like three strikes and you're out. First you get a slap on the wrist. Next you may get three to five years in prison. Finally, you get ten to fifteen years for a third offense. Like my mother, if you gave severe punishment from the start, you would deter repeated future behavior. I call it compassionate law and order.

Chapter Three

Black Lives Matter

The Black Lives Matter movement reminds me of the movie *The Color Purple*. When Oprah Winfrey's character hits the white lady in the town square, she launches an avalanche of white hatred. The crowd hit her and spat on her, and the sheriff busted her head with the butt of his pistol. This reminds me of when a black person kills a white person today, except it is done through the media. The black person is usually denigrated to a point where he or she is less than human. I am not justifying either side of the argument, but it appears that most individuals cannot put themselves in the other's shoes.

The other day, three black youths beat and ridiculed a young man to the point where it was disgraceful and shameful. The three black youths got more bad press than the young white racist who killed nine people in a church vigil.

Most people are not cynical about the justice process. They really believe that the courts eventually get it right when it comes to justice. But justice is not an instant process. The process is time consuming. It may not be your generation that enjoys the fruit of your labor, but sometimes setting a precedent is more beneficial than immediate reward. The mothers involved in these tragedies are not going to agree but rest assured that their children are not dying and getting hurt in vain. Their youths are dying and giving more awareness to a complex issue.

Chapter Four

You Lie

In front of the world during an address to the nation and the world, Barack Obama was told, "You lie." Obama is no stranger to controversy. The man's wife was made fun of because to some she was overweight. Her dignity and grace shown to the public after such rude and obnoxious comments reflect her magnanimous personality. Obama showed the same grace his wife displayed in dealing with this controversial issue.

Barack was so presidential when the comment was made. He kept his momentum during his address; his composure was that of Abraham Lincoln's, a man who argued for the abolition of slavery in America. The congressman who made the comment did not want to answer for his rude outburst. Instead, he retracted it like the true coward most bullies are. Remember that a bully is always tough in a crowd, but alone, he or she is a weak and pathetic creature. The representative who yelled, "You lie" was later admonished and sanctioned.

Chapter Five

Global Warming (Climate Control)

Today I read a story that the earth's temperature is two degrees higher than last year. It has risen over the last three years. With all his will, Barack Obama put together the most aggressive climate-control program measures. For the past eight years, he invested heavily in the alternative energy program—solar and wind technology—making the United States the greenest it has ever been. Still, the efforts have not made a dent in our dependence on fossil fuel. This has been a source of criticism from the left that he is not being aggressive enough and from the right that he is hindering free enterprise.

I live in California, where the problem of climate control manifests itself in many ways. When we hear that the ocean temperature is rising, we notice the various fish washing up onshore. We notice that the drought continues.

We notice how water, a valuable resource, is wasted. We are now on water hours when we can only water our lawns on certain days without the looming penalties if you violate city-ordinance measures. We have no snow in the mountains. This contributes to the drought.

The global community has come to France to discuss global warming and climate control. Our president, Donald Trump, has vowed to kill any act that would limit the amount of fossil-fuel usage to reduce the carbon footprint.

Our children must inherit a planet that has its natural resources. The planet needs to be free of acid rain, and the soil must be clean to ensure that food resources are not contaminated. Our country must lead the world in this effort, and this cannot be seen as a side or trivial issue.

Chapter Six

The Predicate of a False Change

When Barack Obama wrote that change has come to America, he was not dreaming of the false narrative of change that has come to America today. As a professor of organizational change, I never thought I would weigh in on the political climate of change. There have been revolutionary changes, industrial changes, and computer-age change. Political change is not what I am known for. We all, as Americans, have been engaged in the political climate that is Donald Trump. Who knew that the man was so thin skinned that a couple of jokes from Obama would entice him to run for the presidency.

Donald Trump decided that day to run for president, and what is this false narrative that I am talking about? The idea that the majority wins in an election. Hillary Clinton beat the pants off Donald Trump in every aspect of what has been the norm for the presidency. First, she beat him in experience. As secretary of state, she played a key role in some big decisions in the Obama administration—the death of Osama bin Laden, the automobile-industry come-back, and sanctions on Russia and North Korea, to name a few.

She beat Donald Trump in all three debates hands down. Clearly, he was no match for her wit and prepared-ness. If a crisis were to hit America, I suspect that Donald Trump would look like George Bush at the school with the kindergarten students. One can only assess how the bully will react when you stand up to him.

Finally, she beat him with the popular vote. Close to three million more people voted for Hillary Clinton than Donald Trump. The Russian interference practically made a mockery of our democratic system. The FBI director, Comey, bore some of the blame for his pure dissidence. Hillary should not be wondering why she lost but how Donald Trump won. Take a close look at the mayor of New York, who was already talking about victory early on the night of the election, even before many of the west-ern states had come in. Looking at the antics of Flynn, Tillerson, and others may reveal how the election was won.

In keeping with the false narrative of change, Donald Trump has promised America more jobs. Unemployment is at about 5 percent, which is good for most presidents; even Clinton had 4.4 percent at one time, and Reagan had

5 percent. Barack Obama promised jobs and delivered. Hillary followed his lead and continued the same program. What some are not identifying with is that the jobs they once had in coal mines and factories are pretty much obsolete. Americans have to come to grips with the fact that they are going to have to reeducate themselves to get the jobs of the future.

What has to happen for this false narrative of American jobs to dissipate? Americans have to lace up those bootstraps like the greatest generation and get to work. Many blacks have heard for years, "Nothing is given; you have to earn your keep." What I can tell from the coal miners of Kentucky and West Virginia and the union laborers in Pennsylvania, Wisconsin, and Ohio is that they are waiting for something from the past. Education is the real change; seek it to get a hold of your future.

Chapter Seven

Slavery

During the run-up to the election, a statement was made that the Affordable Care Act was akin to slavery and Nazi Germany. It appeared that Barack Obama had the IRS attack citizens to extort money from them to fund a program that was not wanted by the people. Sixty-eight million more people voted for Hillary Clinton than Donald Trump. If one needs to justify the public opinion on Barack Obama's signature bill, one only needs to look at the voting numbers for Hillary Clinton and Donald Trump.

America has come to grips with the Affordable Care Act. One of my son's friends made the statement that he is so glad Obama is not going to be president of the United States anymore. He and his Obamacare are going out the door. My son asked the question, "Well, who do you have for your insurance?" He said he had the Affordable Care Act and that all the freeloaders on Obamacare will go back to not having health care. My son explained to him that the

Affordable Care Act is one in the same as Obamacare. The young man had three kids all under the age of thirteen. He said, "I guess my kids won't have health care because I do not want Obamacare." What is it that makes a man make such a decision? Even at the expense of his kids' health, it is not worth supporting something that he and his family are benefiting from, but Barack Obama made this dreadful bill designed only to destroy America.

Chapter Eight

Thirty-Three Thousand E-mails

When Donald Trump called for the Russians to find the thirty-three thousand e-mails from Hillary Clinton's private server, this was unprecedented—a candidate for the president of the United States openly calling for a former secretary of state to be a victim of cyberterrorism. This is treason by most standards. Barack Obama calling for the Russians to hack Senator Cain would have been nothing but treason to Republicans. The ready-made excuse for every issue that Donald Trump violates is that he is not a politician, and he doesn't understand these issues. This is a very dangerous situation for the country to be in.

Over the years, I have applied for plenty of jobs; there has never failed to be a ready-made excuse from those in the position to hire. Although I have the education for the job, I lack the experience factor that comes with being a director. This statement may have been true in some circumstances; however, I'd find out that the person who got the job was less qualified than me.

Getting back to treason, the Russians did not hack Hillary Clinton's e-mail, but they did hack the Democratic leader's e-mail. A sequence of some rather embarrassing facts came out that made Clinton seem untrustworthy and like she would betray those who support her in a minute for her career.

Barack Obama is believed to have had details regarding Russian hacking, and he elected not to interfere with the election circumstances. Republicans would have gone crazy if he had interfered, and Democrats are just as mad that he elected not to interfere, especially after the FBI director did exactly what the law requires one not to do, which was to not inject himself into the election.

I was asked at work if I supported Barack's decision. You see, I am the token Democrat. I said that Barack Obama was wrong not to tell the public, but what I know is that he would have gotten lambasted if he had done so. The one guy at work who called me "the token black" said, "If you or I had violated handling secret material like Hillary Clinton had done, we would have been punished to the utmost." But he was talking about at our level. Name one person at her level whom anyone has ever questioned about this circumstance before. There has always been a standard that we subordinates have to operate at twice of those at the corporate level. He said, "That does not make it right." So he is saying that Donald Trump's excuse that he is not a politician is not valid.

Chapter Nine

Unemployment Rate

The unemployment rate fell to 4.4 percent under Bill Clinton and 5.3 percent under Ronald Reagan. These presidents were considered two of the best. The difference between them and Obama is that they never had a congress openly state that they would be one-term presidents. They did not have members of Congress openly engage in a super conspiracy to ensure that the executive branch was less powerful than the other two branches of government.

Obama inherited a free-fall economy. The country was losing twenty thousand jobs a month. The unemployment rate was at 10 percent. People were starting to get discouraged and leave the job market. Times were changing when it came to energy jobs. Gasoline was almost five dollars a gallon. People were upset and wanted change. Obama put a stop to the free fall; he reinvested in America with education and the automobile industry. He quickly offered confidence to the free market by hiring a new treasurer. He lowered interest, and the economy began to bounce back. He shored up some of the loopholes when it came to finance. Many of the scammers in the white-collar world were brought to justice. He made it more advantageous to do business in the United States versus carrying jobs overseas.

Month after month, we have had significant job growth. Our current rate is 5 percent job growth, which is a little lower than Reagan and a little higher than Clinton.

Chapter Ten

NAFTA

The North American Free Trade Agreement came up during this election because Donald Trump stated that the American worker has been hindered due to US involvement in this and other agreements. Obama was not part of the team that negotiated this deal, but the media and the Republican party made it seem so. Their disagreement with Trans- Pacific Partnership (TPP) was based on the fact that so many jobs were lost to Mexico and Canada for an agreement that benefited other countries.

Donald Trump, in his "make America great again" rhetoric, is disavowing our participation in TPP. Many of our country's manufacturing jobs have left for Mexico, where the labor is cheaper. This forced our country to make more of a service-oriented industry.

The Clinton administration amended the agreement in agriculture and transportation to allow more agriculture from Mexico to enter our borders. This reduced the cost of farmers' profits, forcing the US government to give farmers subsidies to keep them afloat. The transportation industry was impacted by allowing Mexico's trucks to transport goods further into the United States. The unintended circumstances were that the drug trade became more prevalent. It soon became overwhelming to check every truck going through checkpoints. By simple math, a majority of drugs were going to make it past the checkpoints.

I am a free-trade supporter, but I look forward to a plan that can bring back meaningful work to the United States. The manufacturing of goods in the United States can bring work to the public. I remember when we were the best at building televisions. I remember that when it came to appliances, we were the leader of the free world. A movement back to this can bring many jobs to our nation.

Chapter Eleven

North Korea

We all thought something was wrong with Dennis Rodman when he went to North Korea to play a basketball game against the North Koreans. We were not wrong. It turns out that Dennis is one in the same as the leader of North Korea. The two are similar in that they are both not playing with a complete deck of cards. Republicans tortured Obama over Dennis's decision to play an ambassadorial role for the United States with one of its sworn enemies. The country is part of the Bush administration's axis of evil.

North Korea has been sanctioned by the United States and the rest of the world because of its continued efforts to obtain nuclear weapons that can reach the United States. Year after year, when I was in the military, we would be on exercises to monitor North Korea's testing of their long-range missile capabilities. Year after year, the missile would fail, and the country would be back to the drawing board. The last missile tests were unsatisfactory, but there were some successes in distance. The country is getting close to perfecting its technology.

China, North Korea's neighbor, must move to keep North Korea under wraps. North Korea must find a way to join the rest of the world and abandon its strategy to become nuclear capable—or else. Kim Jong-un's egotistical, maniacal personality, which fits this strategy of being nuclear capable at the expense of his people, is absurd. The man believes he can play basketball so well that he could play in the NBA. The man believes he can beat Serena Williams in tennis. The man's personality has allowed his people to starve at the expense of pursuing nuclear technology.

Chapter Twelve

Iran

The Iranian deal was based on four principles. The Republicans went bonkers when they first heard that the United States was negotiating with who they believed were terrorists. Never mind that Bush negotiated with Saudi Arabia, the home of the majority of men who flew the plane into the World Trade Center buildings. I agreed with Bush at the time, and I agree with the premise behind Obama's policy. According to intelligence reports, Iranians were only two to five years away from having a full nuclear weapon. If we did not engage with the country, we would be sitting with a nuclear missile site ready to launch at Israel. This would put the world on ransom.

We brought the plan to bear on enrichment: Iran's enrichment capacity, enrichment level, and stockpile will be limited for specified durations. There will be no enrichment facilities other than Natanz. Iran is allowed to conduct research and development on centrifuges with an agreed scope and schedule. The Iranians will reprocess the heavy-water facility in Arak with the help of international ventures; it will be redesigned and modernized to a heavy-water research reactor with no weapon-grade plutonium by-products. The spent fuel will be exported; there will be no reprocessing.

The Iranians will be monitored. Iran agreed to the IAEA procedure, which enhanced access by modern technologies to clarify past and present issues. The Iranians will have sanctions. When the IAEA verifies Iran's implementation of its key nuclear commitments, the European Union will terminate all nuclear-related economic sanctions. The United States will cease the application of all nuclear-related secondary economic and financial sanctions. The UN Security Council will endorse this agreement with a resolution that terminates all previous nuclear-related resolutions and incorporate certain restrictive measures for a mutually agreed-upon period of time.

Chapter Thirteen

Syria

It was the president of Syria who clamped down on his people's freedoms. The people of Syria were becoming more and more sympathetic to Western civilization's way of life. In an effort to move past this, the president started to limit the use of the Internet and limit some Muslim traditions. This angered the people, and a backlash against the government developed. The country broke out into a civil war. At one point, the people were starting to gain on the government, and the president warned of the use of chemical weapons.

Obama stepped in and offered a red line against the president. Obama did not enforce his own red line simply because, on one hand, the Republicans did not support him with a resolution to commit acts of war against Syria. On the other hand, the Republicans criticized Obama for not enforcing the red line. Obama could have gone to battle based on his power to protect the American people.

The people were weary of war, and he had a hard time getting them to support an act of war. His reputation suffered a blow. From that point on, the Republicans would label the man as weak even though he tried to get congressional support to take action. The consequences of this lack of action would rear their heads again under the Trump administration.

Chapter Fourteen

Standing Rock

South Dakota was an issue during the 2016 election campaign because of the oil pipeline. The Native American gained much support in their efforts to fight against a pipeline being run through sacred land. The issue for those who support the pipeline is that it will provide jobs to the public, which are much needed. However, these jobs should not come at the expense of Native American communities.

The other issue that came to view was a law-and-order message. People should not have the right to stand in front of vehicles, which impacts on our right to free assembly. The other side of the issue is much more concrete: the idea that the pipeline will impact the environment if there is an oil spill. The largest issue is whether or not the reservation is a free country and if eminent domain comes into play for private companies. True to this issue is that the Army Corps of Engineers stated that the pipeline does not serve the need of any military application.

The courts will have to decide the official outcome of this ever-growing issue. A stay was issued to halt any further action until after the election. Our intention is not to show preference, but in this case, we stand with standing rock!

Chapter Fifteen

Equal Pay for Women

The glass ceiling for women was nearly shattered when Hillary Clinton came close to winning the presidency. The candidate had three million more votes than Donald Trump. She championed a campaign that promoted her fight for women to be more represented in the US Senate and House of Representatives.

Women are reported to make seventy-seven cents on the dollar compared to their male counterparts in the same jobs. We see this glass ceiling in application. The women in the military put their lives on the line the same as the men do. They are entitled to a process that allows them to advance to the same ranks. The issue is moving in the right direction with the evidence that Clinton was so close.

We as a people should look forward to the day when we have a strong female leader who has the compassion of a dove but the tenacious leadership of an eagle.

Chapter Sixteen

Russia

Under the Obama administration, Russia was seen as a clear and present danger to the United States. It is the country with the most nuclear weapons, second only to America. The country fell apart during the early eighties. The Cold War proved to be an effective strategy. Russia focused mainly on trying to keep up with the United States rather than focusing on its people. Outlying countries in the Soviet Union that saw the problem of the central government having too much power and little or no resources brought about the country's downfall.

Today, Putin has been accused of poisoning his rivals. He has invaded his neighbors and launched a propaganda campaign against Europe and now the United States. I fought for years to ensure that Russia was isolated from the rest of the civilized countries. I find it a mistake to put the country on the United Nations council as well as to lift sanctions against a known enemy for the simple fact that Putin called Trump a friend. Russia has no use for democracy. The only idea here is to allow them to get closer to our technology and to grow Russia back to its so-called glory days of the Soviet Union.

Chapter Seventeen

Israel

The two-state solution between Israel and Palestine has been promulgated since the eighties. I want to make it clear that I am firmly behind Israel and its security. The country has what I believe an extra duty to protect its people from persecution. The Nazis have ensured Israel a place in our hearts where we want to support that country even with its flaws. I have watched the process for peace; for years, every president has supported Israel unequivocally. They have supported this process even at the peril of their own two-state solution. Israel has no incentive to sign an accord that would limit its growth when it knows that the negotiating chair has no support of its people to do so.

Obama upped the stakes to ensure that Israel has peace with Palestine. He gave Israel over $30 billion to secure its security. He was undermined by the Republicans and the Israeli prime minister. Obama truly wanted to get a peace deal. The problem was that he had to hold Israel's feet to the fire. The prime minister did not understand that he had to actually make a concession to make the deal happen. No other president had pushed Israel to the table to legitimately get a deal done. Israel launched a phony war against the Palestinians to move away from the talks.

Chapter Eighteen

Harry Reid

"Truth to Power" was the nickname of the Senator from Nevada. Harry Reid had the reputation of being very antagonist to Republicans. Republicans were extremely upset with him for passing the Affordable Care Act. The law has given insurance to over twenty million people, who previously would not have had that protection.

Harry Reid was the first person of prominence to call Republicans out for their initial stance to hold Obama to a one-term presidency. The Republicans went on to act in the exact same that way Harry Reid stated, obstructing Obama in every aspect of governing. They even went against previous policies that they approved, all to give Obama a difficult time.

Harry went on the Senate floor and called Obama a historic figure and indicated that Obama would go down as one of America's most successful presidents. The man had zero scandals while being president. During the past eight years, no foreign terrorist organization has successfully planned and executed an attack on our homeland. Plots had been disrupted. Terrorists like Osama bin Laden had been taken off the battlefield. Obama wrote about his diplomatic milestones like the Iran nuclear deal and the warm relationship with Cuba as well as getting the unemployment rate below 5 percent and passing the Affordable Care Act. He prevented the privatizing of Medicare and Social Security. He also led key criminal-justice reform.

Chapter Nineteen

Male versus Female Stamina

The most repulsive thing I have ever heard in a debate was when one candidate referred to the size of his hands in regards to his private parts. He said that he did not have a problem with that. "You can ask around." A man who grabs women by the pussy and openly talks about his prowess with women is not worthy of the presidency. I guess our traditions are, as some have said, a technique to discourage others from seeking the presidency. My thought process on this is, *What if Obama would have made those statements? Would he have been given such a reprieve?*

If you compare Hillary to Trump, she looked like a young law student in comparison. She was lively and energetic. She smiled. She was prepared. This is the reason Trump and the Republicans kept attacking her for looking tired. She has health problems. The concept was another alternate truth. Trump even suggested that Hillary looked tired when she left the stage. The truth is that Trump looked and acted as if he was on drugs. I can only imagine what one has to take to have that much of a nonreaction to questions.

The comment by Trump that Hillary is a "nasty woman" is the kind of insult a batterer would say when a woman is fighting back, and the batterer is frustrated. He wants so much to intimidate through hyper reaction. He wants her to submit to him on the basis of his looks. He wants her to flinch from the movement of his hands. He wants her to know that she knows what is coming if she does not submit to his demands.

Chapter Twenty

Abortion

The most courageous act a woman can make is the decision of what to do with her own body. The Republicans call this act immoral. They use isolated incidents of outrageous abortions to justify why they don't belong in someone else's life.

I am very religious, and I share the idea of not having abortions. This immoral act will be judged by the superior being that the Republicans are forcing on others. They say they believe in life. But they attempt to make a law where a motorist has the right to run a person over with a car if that person blocks traffic. What is more absurd—that or the Republican belief that a woman should be forced to carry a child in the case of rape and incest? If a woman wants to carry a rapist's baby, she should; but if she chooses not to, there should be adequate medical conditions set up for her health concerns and moral welfare.

Chapter Twenty-One

Domestic Agenda

Every election-cycle candidate says that capitalism is being suppressed by high taxes, regulations, and social-welfare programs. Every election cycle, middle-class America has the trickle-down theory shoved down its throat.

What I want white, southern Americans to understand is that every election cycle, Republicans offer you trickle down and more jobs. This does not happen, and you get angrier and angrier at black and Mexican Americans. You allow the Republican elite to use you in their Ponzi schemes. You are going to get jobs as soon as we get those black and Mexican Americans under control.

The truth is that blacks are getting educated. They are seeking technology like no other race. They are making marks in areas where it was thought that they could never achieve. The military has been a vehicle of leadership that is preparing more blacks and people of color with skills that were once unavailable. Is that what Donald Trump represents—a fight back against the upward mobility of others? We as Americans are better than our petty differences. We all must get on the boat of education and innovation, which will take us to prosperity, freedom, and a nation full of hope.

As for regulations, we must understand that too many can stifle the economy. Is this a myth? My economics classes taught that regulation fuels the economy. For example, when you have a business, you need to get resources to ensure that you pass government standards. This concept leads to more goods being purchased or smaller companies being needed to specialize in certain tasks. This creates a multiple-faceted approach to solving a problem, not a monolithic one. This fuels the marketplace with more goods required and more small businesses. The concept of deregulation often is a boost to the economy, but the problem is that we cannot sustain the economy for long periods of time. Deregulation often leads to more deaths and accidents that lead to less consumer confidence. The economy usually slows or decreases.

The last drain on the domestic agenda is social programs. Social programs in a capitalist system are frowned upon by right-wing conservatives. Under these social programs, items such as Social Security and Medicare cannot be sustained and are a drain on the economy. The military is exempt from this "drain on the economy" because it is mainly made up of conservatives.

Chapter Twenty-Two

Education

Private versus public education has always been a topic at every debate. This country debates the concepts of public education most regularly. It is a fair idea that public education is funded the same as private education. The government gives about three thousand dollars per student per year to fund each person's education. This leads to more schools being antiquated and having overcrowded classrooms.

The charter school movement has lessened this impact. Charter schools have the ability to take government funds and also have the parents contribute to the education of the students. This provides better staffing and less crowded schools. The new deal with leadership in this area is to share education.

The idea that schools have to go to the US Department of Education to get accreditation has been a source of contention for Republican educators. They believe that states should be able to come up with their own standards. We had this before, during the days of the Jim Crow South.

Chapter Twenty-Three

Blame It on Obama

What I have seen in every president, I have borne witness to from Jimmy Carter to George Bush. I have never questioned whether a president loves this country or not. I have seen honor in all presidents. I have seen leadership in times of turmoil. I have seen charisma, the kind that brings our country to a willingness to think "America first."

I do not think "America first" means what Trump is touting. His type of selfishness is that of a child in a sandbox. He wants the whole sandbox to himself, so he pushes other kids out. In other words, he takes his basketball and goes home as soon as he loses. This type of selfishness cannot win the day.

Obama has all the qualities of a great leader, and more, he has the one leadership characteristic that most cannot gauge. It is called compassion. Compassion makes you love others to the point where you protect them at almost any cost. His is not a phony compassion. One can see this in the speeches he delivered about the school shooting in Connecticut. One can see it when he said that he could have been Trayvon Martin. You could definitely see it in his ability to track down Osama bin Laden and deliver a blow for the world. His compassion for those involved in 9/11 would not let him forget the many who were sacrificed that day.

So, Obama, I blame it all on you. Your leadership of selflessness and compassion has really made America great again because you put the American people in front of profit.

Conclusion

Reflection

So to reflect on the Obama presidency, during his last address at White House Correspondents' Association dinner, he dropped the microphone. Ironically, in the movie *Coming to America*, Eddie Murphy drops the microphone and walks offstage. One of the audience members makes the comment, "That boy is good. He sure is good." I guess Obama was saying the same thing: "I came, I conquered, and I delivered probably the best example of leadership that this country has had since John F. Kennedy."

Obama had been in the forefront of many issues in the 2016 election. He was not running for office, but he made a statement that he believed he would have won a third term if he could have run. Based on his accomplishments, he might have been correct.

I am a Democrat who works in a very Republican, conservative environment. My thoughts on the idea of a third term are mixed. I, too, was encouraged by the polls.

However, I saw the ugly truth about our country and the way that many whites were feeling. Many of them had pure hatred for Obama. One gentleman asked my opinion on Obama. I said he was OK and that he was doing some great things for the country. The coworker went absolutely nuts. He even threatened that I should not have a job at the place because I made such a statement.

After that statement, everything that Obama did was amplified in my workplace. I was also told that I was our token Democrat. The implication was that I was not qualified for the position. Granted, in the military, I was an enlisted service warfare specialist, aviation warfare specialist, and master training specialist with an associate degree in electrical/electronic technology, a bachelor in information technology, a master's in business, and a doctorate in business. Previously, I worked in one industry, where I completed nineteen out of nineteen projects on time and on budget. My credentials speak for me.

Despite Obama's qualifications and the deeds that he performed, to many he was not acceptable because he was black and or he was a bleeding liberal.